JOURNEY TO A

The Immigrants of Ellis Island

Julie Anne Savage

Green Apple Lessons Publishing
Image Credits: New York Public Library, Digital Collections
ISBN - 13: 978-1-0879-8507-7

Dedication

This book is dedicated to my beloved grandfather, Emil John Ambrite. Emil's parents immigrated from Hungary to the United States in the early 1900s. Papa endured great hardships, including being raised in a Catholic orphanage after his father abandoned the family and his mother could no longer support her children. By the grace of God, he overcame his struggles and went on to live the American dream. He passed on a sincere love of God and country to his children and grandchildren. This book is written in his honor.

Who Are Immigrants?

Immigrants are people who move to a new country to live. In the late 1800s and early 1900s, many people left their home countries to come to America in search of a better life.

The reasons why they left were as varied as the people themselves. Some left due to religious or political persecution. Others left because of war or famine. People yearned for freedom and the ability to work, own property, and make a better life for themselves and their families. This is called the American Dream.

Did You Know?

The term "American Dream" was coined by an American writer named James Truslow Adams. Adams wrote "life should be better and richer and fuller for everyone, with opportunity for each according to ability or achievement regardless of social class or the circumstances of birth."

What did people bring on their journey to America?

Immigrants left behind other family members, friends and sacrificed a great deal in their pursuit of freedom. Suitcase space was limited so people could only bring essentials such as clothing, and a few of their most treasured personal possessions.

Many immigrants packed clothing, a Bible, family heirlooms, wool blankets, money, musical instruments, pictures of family and small toys for their children. Tradesmen often brought their work tools in hopes they would find work in America.

Did You Know?

Some immigrants hid garden seeds in the lining of their clothing. For these immigrants, gardens provided a sense of home and a source of future food security.

What Is Ellis Island?

Ellis Island was an immigration processing center, located between New York and New Jersey. It sits at the mouth of the Hudson River. Ellis Island served as the gateway for people who wanted to enter America.

Ellis Island was nicknamed the "Island of Hope." Millions of people passed through Ellis Island, with an average of 2000 people being processed per day. Each immigrant who passed through Ellis Island had dreams and hopes for a brighter future and a fresh start in a new land.

Did You Know?

Over 40% of all Americans today are descendants from the men, women and children that passed through Ellis Island.

Who Was Annie Moore?

Annie Moore was the first immigrant to come through the newly built Ellis Island Immigration Station on January 1, 1892. Annie was just a teenager when she traveled with her two younger brothers from Ireland. They were seeking reunification with their parents, who came to America four years earlier.

The siblings traveled on a steamship called the S.S. Nevada. It arrived too late one evening for the passengers to be processed. The next morning, the travelers were sent to Ellis Island to be the first group processed at the newly built Immigration Station.

As the ship docked, Annie was the very first passenger to disembark. Annie was greeted with a warm welcome to America and a $10 gold piece. This was a souvenir gift for being the first registered immigrant to arrive through the newly opened station.

A bronze statue of Annie Moore, created by Irish sculptor Jeanne Rynhart.

Portraits of American Immigrants

Albanian Man

Ladies from Guadeloupe,
the French Caribbean Island

Children from Finland

A Danish Man

Three Dutch Women

Bavarian Man

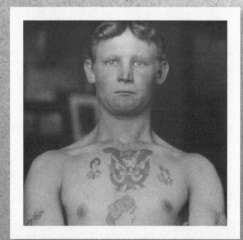

A German Stowaway

A Soldier from Greece

Jewish Grandma

Portraits of American Immigrants

English Family

Turkish Family

Hungarian Gypsies

German Family

Scottish Boys

Welcome to America!

After the long sea journey, one of the first things immigrants saw while entering the New York Harbor was the Statue of Liberty. Lady Liberty symbolizes freedom and a chance for a better life and future.

**Give me your tired, your poor
Your huddled masses yearning to breathe free
The wretched refuse of your teeming shore
Send these, the homeless, tempest-tost to me
I lift my lamp beside the golden door!**

Poet Emma Lazarus, "The New Colossus," 1883
Inscribed beneath the Statue of Liberty in 1903

How did immigrants get to Ellis Island?

Most immigrants traveled by large steam ships from Europe to Ellis Island. Many people came from small European villages which made the commute an even longer journey.

Families left their villages by wagon or train and headed to a major port city, such as Amsterdam, Holland or Bremen, Germany. Many arrived a few days before the date of their departure and stayed in immigrant hotels located near the port. Once they boarded the ship, the journey to America could take up to two weeks, depending on the weather and their point of departure.

Wealthy people often stayed in first class cabins on the ship. Most travelers stayed in the bottom portion of the ship, called the steerage. The conditions in steerage were cramped, overcrowded and smelly. Steerage passengers slept in narrow bunks in heavily crowded rooms. Many people became seasick during the long ocean journey. The average price for a steerage ticket in the early 1900s with around $30. Many immigrants received prepaid tickets from family members already in America.

What happened upon arrival to Ellis Island?

Once docked, immigrants were shuttled on ferries to Ellis Island to be processed for entry into the United States. Steam ships would dock in Manhattan because the waters surrounding Ellis Island were too shallow for the large barges. Once they arrived at the Immigration Station, interpreters would come out and explain the next steps to the immigrants in their native languages. Some Ellis Island interpreters spoke up to six different languages.

Did You Know?

Some immigrants reported that dock workers tried to bribe them into giving them money to bypass the inspection process to enter the country. Corruption at Ellis Island was not a common practice, but unfortunately did occur.

Who underwent medical inspections?

All newcomers to America had to pass medical inspections to ensure that they were not bringing any diseases into the country. Immigrants were taken to the Great Hall, where they registered and were given a brief health exam. Doctors checked for contagious diseases, such as yellow fever, tuberculosis, and lice.

The doctors used a piece of chalk to mark the clothing of immigrants that they suspected had medical problems. These people were removed from the line and taken into a new area for further inspection.

The "button hook men" were doctors who checked immigrants' eyes for a highly contagious eye disease called trachoma. Trachoma often caused blindness and sometimes death. The doctors would use a button hook to turn the immigrants' eyelids inside out to check for signs of the disease. Trachoma caused more immigrants deportations than any other illness or disease.

Did You Know?

Ellis Island doctors wore outfits that looked like military uniforms. The doctors were commissioned officers of the United States Public Health Service. Their appearance likely was an intimidating sight for new and confused immigrants arriving from other countries.

What were the legal inspections?

Immigrants who passed medical inspections next underwent a brief legal examination. This questioning process verified the items of personal information that was provided by the immigrants and contained on the ship's manifest records.

Inspectors verified each person's name, age, occupation, and their point of departure. Inspectors only had a few minutes to decide whether each immigrant was "clearly and beyond a doubt" entitled to land in America.

The United States government did not want anyone to enter who would be a charge or burden to the state. Persons with severe debt, legal, medical problems or criminal histories were likely detained. In a few rare cases, they were deported back to their home country.

Out of the millions of immigrants who came through Ellis Island, less than 2% were detained or deported. Most people passed through Ellis Island within three to five hours and were free to enter America and begin their new lives.

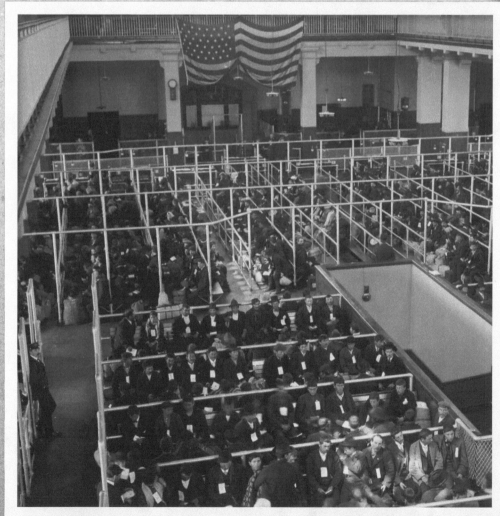

Did You Know?

Ellis Island had both a dormitory and a dining hall. The dining hall served detained immigrants three free meals a day. Typical fare included beef stew, herring, potatoes, bread, and stewed prunes. Kosher meals were provided to Jewish guests. Other immigrants passing through Ellis Island could purchase sack lunches for $1, which often contained a sandwich and fruit.

Where did the immigrants go after leaving Ellis Island?

Many people stayed. Others traveled to railroad stations in New Jersey, to take trains to other regions of the United States. Most immigrants started immediately looking for permanent jobs and housing.

After settling into their new destinations, many immigrants kept alive their rich heritage, food, cultures, and traditions. Most immigrants, however, wanted to be known as Americans first. This is called assimilation. Assimilation is the process of assuming the values, behaviors, and beliefs of a new people group.

Did You Know?

The United States is known as the great American "melting pot" because many cultures came together to become something new and great. The phrase was coined in 1908 by Israel Zangwill, a British author. It was first used as a metaphor to describe America's union of many nationalities, cultures, and ethnicities.

What is Ellis Island used for today?

Ellis Island is no longer used as an immigration processing center. It officially closed in November of 1954. This was due to a steady decline in the numbers of people immigrating to America. The Immigration Act of 1924 restricted American immigration and allowed immigrants to be processed at American embassies in their home country of origin.

In 1976, Ellis Island became a tourist center. It's now an immigration museum and part of the National Park Service along with the Statue of Liberty.

The American Family Immigration History Center is located on the first floor of the Ellis Island Immigration Museum. This center helps visitors conduct research of family members who came through as immigrants to Ellis Island.

Why is Ellis Island important?

Ellis Island will always be significant because it served as the gateway for over 12 million people to enter our country. The Island of Hope was the first stop for many on the long journey to forging a new life in the United States of America.

Did You Know?

The patriotic anthem "God Bless America" was composed by an immigrant. Irving Berlin left his home in Siberia for America when he was only five years old. He became a prolific songwriter and penned these words:

God bless America, land that I love
Stand beside her and guide her
Through the night with the light from above

From the mountains to the prairies
To the oceans white with foam
God bless America, my home sweet home!